SUPER SMART INFORMATION STRATEGIES

BLOG IT!

by Kristin Fontichiaro

CHERRY LAKE PUBLISHING • ANN ARBOR, MICHIGAN

A NOTE TO PARENTS AND TEACHERS: Please remind your children how to stay safe online before they do the activities in this book.

CHERRY LAKE Publishing

A NOTE TO KIDS: Always remember your safety comes first!

Published in the United States of America
by Cherry Lake Publishing
Ann Arbor, Michigan
www.cherrylakepublishing.com

Content Adviser: Gail Dickinson, PhD,
Associate Professor, Old Dominion University,
Norfolk, Virginia

Photo Credits: Cover and page 24, ©iStockphoto.com/LUNAMARINA; page 4,
©iStockphoto.com/gradyreese; page 6, ©Lisa F. Young/Dreamstime.com; page
7, ©Photoeuphoria/Dreamstime.com; page 9, ©MikLav/Shutterstock, Inc.;
page 11, ©Audiolui/Dreamstime.com; page 12, ©Britvich/Dreamstime.com;
page 15, ©Aivolie/Shutterstock, Inc.; page 17, ©Richard Thomas/Dreamstime.
com; page 22, ©Jonathan Ross/Dreamstime.com; page 23, ©Szasz-Fabian Ilka
Erika/Shutterstock, Inc.; page 26, ©Martin Novak/Dreamstime.com; page 28,
©Layland Masuda/Shutterstock, Inc.

Library of Congress Cataloging-in-Publication Data
Fontichiaro, Kristin.
  Blog it! / by Kristin Fontichiaro.
    p. cm. — (Information explorer)
  Includes bibliographical references and index.
  ISBN 978-1-61080-482-0 (lib. bdg.) — ISBN 978-1-61080-569-8 (e-book) —
ISBN 978-1-61080-656-5 (pbk.)
  1. Blogs—Juvenile literature. I. Title.
  TK5105.8884.F66 2012
  006.7'52—dc23   2012009869

Cherry Lake Publishing would like to acknowledge
the work of The Partnership for 21st Century Skills.
Please visit www.21stcenturyskills.org for more information.

Printed in the United States of America
Corporate Graphics Inc.
July 2012
CLFA11

Table of Contents

CHAPTER ONE
Do You Need a Blog?

A blog is a great way to share exciting vacation stories.

Have you ever wanted to share everything you were
doing on a family vacation with your friends back
home? Have you ever wished you could give a sick
classmate details about what was going on in school?
Maybe you're helping your uncle fix up his classic car.
If you could write about each step of the process, then
people in the local car club could follow along.

4

If you like telling people what's happening, then you should think about starting a **blog**. A blog is a special kind of Web site where you can share your thoughts by writing **posts**. Blogging is kind of like writing in a journal or a diary. But most diaries or journals are about keeping your secrets private. Blogs are posted online for anyone to read. You can write every day, every few days, or when something special happens. Blogs let you include videos, photos, and sound recordings along with your words! Each time you add a new post to your blog, it appears at the very top of your Web page. This means that people who visit your blog always see the newest information first.

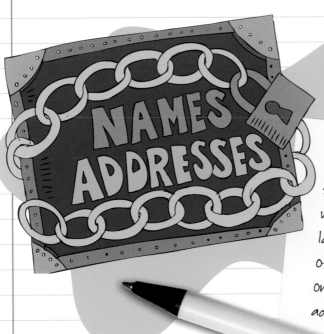

While the Web is almost always safe, keep your privacy in mind so you stay safe. Avoid using your last name as well as the full name of your friends, relatives, school, or sports team. Never give your address or phone number.

Blogs are a great way to let people know what you are doing, thinking about, and planning, right as it is happening. Some people write in the same blog for years and years. Your parents or guardians might keep a long-term blog with photos of you growing up.

Other blogs are kept just for a few months. Maybe your family is renovating your house. You can take turns adding photos and words to describe how the

Your blog could highlight the ways your house is improved during a renovation project.

Many teachers create blogs to keep their students up-to-date on homework assignments and other class news.

house changes each day. Maybe your sports team has a blog for the season. It might remind players when practices are, where the games will be held, and what happened during each game.

Some people use blogs in school. Your teacher might keep a blog to remind you of your homework. You and your classmates might take turns writing blog posts about class news.

There sure are a lot of things you can blog about!

TRY THIS!

What do you want to blog about? Brainstorm a list. Next to each topic, think about whether this is a long-term or short-term topic.

BRAINSTORM

Ask for permission from your parents or guardians before you start to blog. If you are at least 13 years old, you can set up your own blog. If you are not that old yet, ask your parents if they can set up a blog and share the password.

Possible Topics	How Long Would It Last?

To get a copy of this activity, visit www.cherrylakepublishing.com/activities.

CHAPTER TWO
Setting Up Your Blog

Ask a parent or teacher to help you choose the blogging tools that are right for you.

There are lots of ways to set up a blog online for free.

1. If you have your own Web site, most **Web hosts** have blogging tools. You can install these on your site for no extra cost.

2. If you are blogging for a class project, your teacher might use a Web site such as Kidblog (*http://kidblog.org*). It sets up private blogs for each member of the class. You, your teacher, and your classmates can see it, but other people cannot. This is an excellent way to start blogging safely.

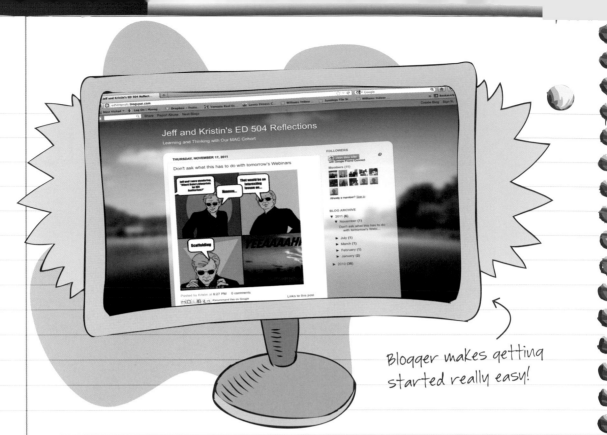

Blogger makes getting
started really easy!

3. If you are blogging for fun, you can use Google's
   Blogger (*www.blogger.com*). Blogger is very
   popular because it is free and easy to use. If
   you have a Gmail account, you can use it to log
   in to Blogger. If not, you'll need to create a new
   account. You can set up as many blogs as you
   want, but it's always easiest to start with one!
   Blogger lets you post photos, **text**, and video.

4. The most powerful free blogging tool is
   WordPress (*http://wordpress.com*). WordPress
   lets you upload audio files. This is not possible
   on Blogger. WordPress is more complicated than
   most other blogging tools. You can **customize** it
   much more, but Blogger and Kidblog are easier
   for beginners to use.

Once you have an account at a blogging site, you need to choose a title for your blog. Sometimes people create titles that include their names, like Grace's Ideas or Jeff's Amazing Thoughts. Choose your title carefully to set a mood that is funny, thoughtful, or serious. Here are some examples of good blog titles:

- My Journey Through Fourth Grade
- Our Trip to the Grand Canyon
- Come to Our 2012 Block Party!
- Our Class Hamsters Are Growing!

A trip to the Grand Canyon would give you plenty of interesting things to blog about.

Be sure to pick a title that matches your topic. For example, I Love Mac and Cheese could be a great title for a food blog. But it would be a terrible title for a class newsletter! The good news is you can change your blog title at any time.

Now you need to create a **URL** for your blog. This is the address people will type in to visit your blog. If you are using Blogger, you need to think of something that will fit in this blank:

http://_____.blogspot.com

For WordPress, you need to fill in the blank here:

http://_____.wordpress.com

A food blog is a great way to share your experiences with cooking and eating delicious meals.

baby bunnies
little rabbits

Brainstorm a list of possible URLs for your blog, in case your first choice isn't available.

Most people try to make their blog title and their URL as similar as possible. You should brainstorm a few backup possibilities, in case someone has already taken the URL you want. No two Web sites can have the same URL! Try to think of variations, such as 4th instead of fourth, or rabbit instead of bunny. Or use abbreviations, such as bc instead of Battle Creek. Use lowercase letters only.

Let's look at the earlier title examples and give them some sample URLs:

Blog Title	Possible URLs
My Journey Through Fourth Grade	• http://fourthgrade.blogspot.com • http://4thgrade.wordpress.com • http://myjourneythroughfourthgrade.blogspot.com • http://4thgradejourney.wordpress.com
Our Trip to the Grand Canyon	• http://grandcanyontrip.wordpress.com • http://grandcanyontrip2012.blogspot.com • http://gcvacationjuly.wordpress.com
Come to Our 2012 Block Party!	• http://blockpartyinfo.blogspot.com • http://2012blockparty.blogspot.com • http://blockparty.wordpress.com
Our Class Hamsters Are Growing!	• http://ourhamsters.blogspot.com • http://hamstersgrowing.blogspot.com • http://room4hamsters.wordpress.com

When you are choosing your blog title or URL, don't give away personal information. That includes your last name and address.

Now that your blog has been created and named, you should customize its appearance. Every blogging site has many options you can choose from to change the look of your blog. These options are called **templates** or themes. They include different colors and illustrations that can help express your blog's mood, personality, or content. For example, a template with cupcakes on it would be perfect if you want to blog about your school's bake sale. But that same template might look weird if you were blogging about your trip to Niagara Falls!

Imagine you are at Niagara Falls. How would you describe it on your blog?

TRY THIS!

Come up with some possible subjects for your blog. Brainstorm a list of possible titles and URLs. Then think about what colors, images, or designs would be useful for those topics. Now, work with an adult to set up your blog account. Pick a title, URL, and theme.

To get a copy of this activity, visit www.cherrylakepublishing.com/activities.

Hello Bunny!

CHAPTER FOUR
Pre-Search
Before Research

Have you ever seen a bush baby at a zoo?

Quick—what questions do you have about bush babies? How about Demetrios Ypsilantis? Your questions are probably "What's a bush baby?" and "Who is Demetrios Ypsilantis?" Those are both closed questions, but that's all we can ask because we don't know anything about the topics. That happens a lot in school. Sometimes we

└ Austin is one of the biggest cities in Texas.

can't ask great questions because we don't know anything about what we're researching.

Let's pretend that you are going on vacation this
summer, but your parents can't decide where to go. They
are trying to decide between Texas and Michigan. They
also think it might be fun to simply visit another part
of your own state. They want you to do some research
on the places you could visit and the different activities
that are available in each place. Where should you start?
Well, it's always best to start with what you know.

For each state, make a list of things you already know. You probably know a lot about your own state. You've likely studied it in school or looked at it on a map. But imagine that you don't know much about Michigan. You might have a short list, like this:

What I Think I Know About Michigan	Questions I Have	What I've Learned
• shaped like a mitten	• Are the two parts of the state connected?	
• divided into two parts		
• capital is Lansing	• What fun things can we do in the state?	
• Mariposa's dad lives there		

Is that enough for a report? Not yet. But it is definitely a good start. It is pretty interesting that Michigan is divided into two parts and shaped like a mitten. And it's always good to know where a state's capital is. And if Mariposa's dad lives there, maybe he could tell you some things.

There's another great way to start learning when you get stuck on what questions to ask: do some pre-search. When we pre-search, we're telling ourselves, "Hmmm. Before I go searching for details online or in books, I want to know some basics about my topic."

Michigan is home to many beautiful sights.

An encyclopedia is sure to have information about almost any topic you can think of.

One great way to pre-search is to use **encyclopedias**. In a lot of libraries, encyclopedias are sets of books that can take up a foot or more of shelf space. Inside, there is a little bit of information about a lot of different topics: plants, animals, places, people, and history. Many libraries also pay for encyclopedias that you can access online. These are great places to start. The information in encyclopedias is written by experts, so it is very reliable. It also gives you a general overview of the topic, so you can learn enough to ask questions. Ask your librarian for these common encyclopedia brands: World Book, Heinemann First Encyclopedia, Encyclopaedia Britannica, or Grolier Online.

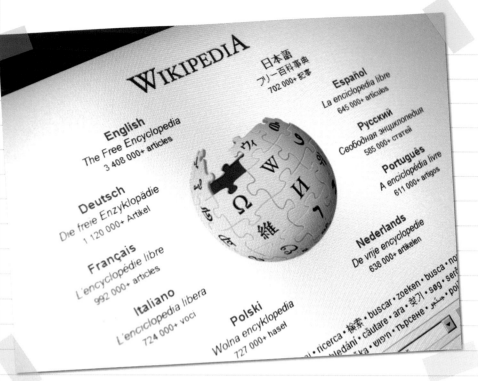

Wikipedia can be a useful place to begin your investigation.

Wikipedia, the biggest encyclopedia in the world, is not written just by experts. Almost anyone can edit it. That's both good and bad. Anybody can contribute, so Wikipedia is a huge collection of information about almost anything. On the other hand, because anybody can change the content, some information might be inaccurate. Smart researchers always use other sources after starting with Wikipedia or other online resources to be sure the information is accurate.

If we look up Michigan in an encyclopedia, we can get a lot of basic information fast. Now our list looks like this:

What I Think I Know About Michigan	Questions I Have	What I've Learned
• shaped like a mitten	• Are the two parts of the state connected?	
• divided into two parts	• Why does Michigan have so many sports teams?	
• capital is Lansing	• Why is the auto industry struggling?	
• Mariposa's dad lives there	• What kinds of cars do they make there?	
• center of struggling U.S. auto industry	• Why does Michigan have so many universities?	
• lots of farms—apples, cherries	• How would we get there from our house?	
• lots of universities and colleges	• Which players made the biggest contributions to the Tigers? Why?	
• lots of sports: Detroit Tigers, Red Wings, Pistons, Lions	• What fun things can we do in the state?	

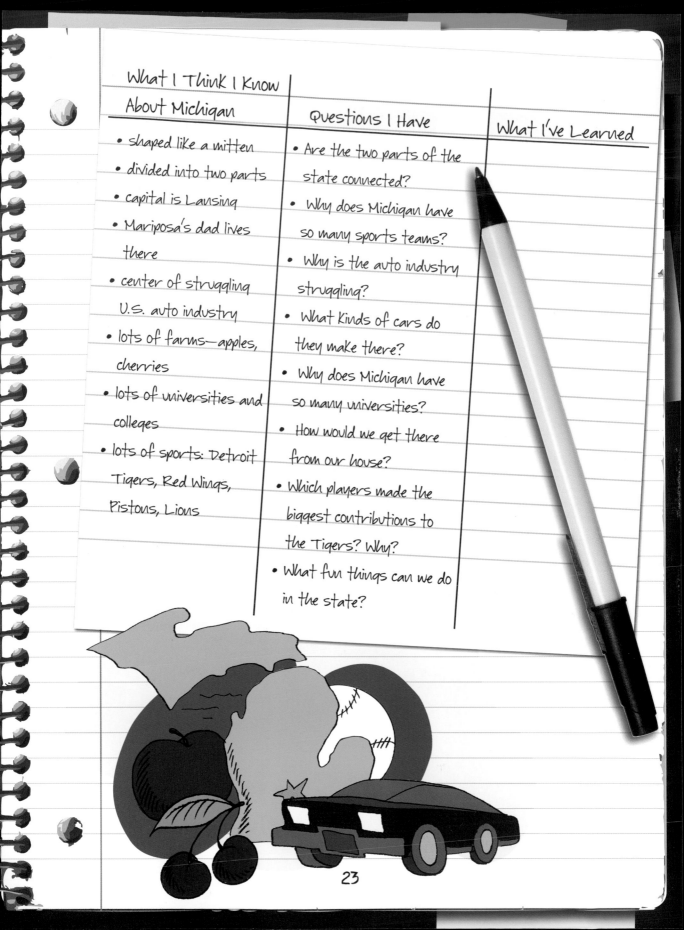

See how many more questions we have now that we know a few more facts? A few minutes of reading an encyclopedia entry can really get you excited about your topic.

Here are tips for how to use any encyclopedia well:

- Use encyclopedias at the beginning of your questioning only.
- Use the section headings and the outline at the beginning to help you skim, or quickly read, the article.

- Look for basic facts and gather keywords you can use when you research with books, Web sites, or experts.
- Make notes about what you have learned.
- Write down new questions as they come up.

- Look at the very bottom of the entry. You might see references or external links. Click on those links, or type the addresses into your Web browser. You'll be able to see the articles or Web pages about the topic that someone else already decided are reliable and useful. That's better than typing your topic into a search engine!

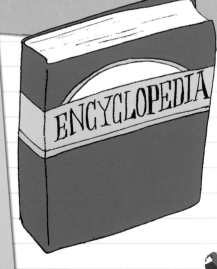

Once you've gotten that basic information, you don't need Wikipedia or any other encyclopedia anymore. Move on to meatier and more interesting articles, Web pages, books, or people!

What I Think I Know	Questions I Have	What I've Learned

TRY THIS!

Fold a large piece of paper in thirds. Make a chart with three columns like the one shown above. Pick a topic you don't know very much about. Brainstorm a list of what you think you know and what questions you have. Then read an encyclopedia entry about that topic. Brainstorm a new list of things you know and compare it to the old one to see how much you've learned!

To get a copy of this activity, visit www.cherrylakepublishing.com/activities.

CHAPTER FIVE
Any More Questions?

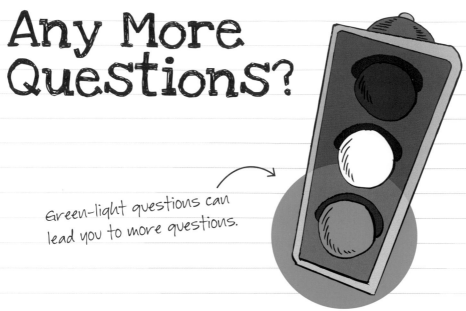

Green-light questions can lead you to more questions.

Now that we've researched different options, we're done, right? Nope! Once you think you've answered the question you asked, you need to **evaluate** your answer. This means you need to look at the question you asked, compare it to the answers you found, and decide whether that information has answered the question or led you to new questions.

When you evaluate your answers, you will usually find new questions that you weren't even aware of! For example, early on in your research about Michigan for your family trip, you might have wondered, "Are there ski resorts there?" Your family loves to downhill ski in the winter. But that would have been a closed question. You may have searched online for "Michigan ski resorts" and discovered that there are both downhill and cross-country ski resorts in Michigan. This might have led to new questions. Maybe you asked yourself, "What's cross-country skiing?" and started a new search. Maybe you asked your parents, "Do you like to cross-country ski? Would you like to learn, or would you rather go downhill skiing?" Or you might have called a cross-country ski resort and asked, "Do you make artificial snow if we plan a trip and it doesn't snow? How do you do that?"

Good questions usually lead you to more questions, which lead you to more learning and exploration. That doesn't mean you goofed up on your questions. It means you are really interested in your topic!

What kind of skiing would you like to try?

⌐ Thomas Edison asked the right questions
to keep us out of the dark!

Sometimes, though, we get stumped, and our
questions seem to have no answers. If that happens,
try adding **synonyms**, or words that mean the same
as your keywords. If you are stumped when searching
for "ski resorts," try "ski companies" or "ski hills." Still
stumped? Try searching for "ski equipment." If you can
find a ski store, there is probably a snowy hill nearby.
Call and ask!

Remember, all over the world, some questions are still
waiting to be answered. Think about scientists or experts.
Their job is to ask questions, all day every day! Imagine
if Thomas Edison had never wondered how to make

electricity into a light. Many people wondered if it was possible, but it was Edison's curiosity that turned a question into an answer. What if Columbus had never wondered if there was another way to sail around the world? Many of our ancestors might never have come to North America.

Questioning is not a once-in-a-while activity for most people. When we learn to ask great questions, we are building skills that we can use for the rest of our lives. We are learning new things and exploring the world around us.

TRY THIS!

Let's put everything we've talked about into practice! Get a small notebook and, before you go to bed at night, write down every question you can think of that came up during the day. You can also carry the notebook with you and write your questions down as soon as they come to mind. When you find an answer, write it down. Create your own personal encyclopedia. And who knows—maybe your questions will lead you to the next big discovery!

MY NOTEBOOK

To get a copy of this activity, visit www.cherrylakepublishing.com/activities.

Glossary

documentaries (dahk-yuh-MEN-tur-eez) films that are about
  real facts, people, and events

encyclopedias (en-sye-kloh-PEE-dee-uhz) books or sets of
  books with information on a wide variety of topics

evaluate (i-VAL-yoo-ate) decide the importance of something
  by thinking about it carefully

keywords (KEE-wurdz) words that can be uses to search for
  information on Web sites

outline (OUT-line) a quick list of the most important ideas in
  a paper or article

references (REF-ruhn-siz) the Web sites, articles, books, and
  other materials that a writer uses to write a report

research (REE-surch) the process of asking questions, finding
  answers, and evaluating those answers

section headings (SEK-shuhn HED-ingz) bold print that tells
  the main idea of the paragraphs about to be read

synonyms (SIN-uh-nimz) words that share a meaning

Find Out More

BOOKS

Rabbat, Suzy. *Find Your Way Online*. Ann Arbor, MI: Cherry
Lake Publishing, 2010.

Truesdell, Ann. *Find the Right Site*. Ann Arbor, MI: Cherry Lake
Publishing, 2010.

Truesdell, Ann. *Fire Away: Asking Great Interview Questions*.
Ann Arbor, MI: Cherry Lake Publishing, 2013.

WEB SITES

Fact Monster
www.factmonster.com
This free, ad-supported site features an almanac, atlas, encyclopedia, dictionary, and thesaurus. It's recommended for kids
ages 8 to 14 as a pre-search site.

Google Search Education Evangelism
https://sites.google.com/site/gwebsearcheducation/
This site offers a set of lessons and strategies for learning to be
a better online searcher.

The Kentucky Virtual Library Presents: How to Do Research
www.kyvl.org/kids/homebase.html
A research map helps guide students through the process of
research, by suggesting questions, what you already know, and
keywords.

Index

Kristin Fontichiaro teaches at the University of Michigan, where scholars, professors, students, and scientists are always asking questions!

About the Authors

Emily Johnson was born in Utah, went to school in Michigan, and is now the librarian at Pledge Harbor School in Dhaka, the capital city of Bangladesh. As she travels the world, she asks lots of questions!

**Jeffersonville Township Public
Library**
P.O. Box 1548
Jeffersonville, IN 47131